SECRETS OF THE SUN

A Closer Look at Our Star

Patricia Barnes-Svarney

RAINTREE
STECK-VAUGHN
PUBLISHERS

A Harcourt Company

Austin · New York
www.steck-vaughn.com

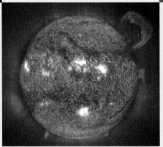

Steck-Vaughn Company

First published 2001 by Raintree Steck-Vaughn Publishers,
an imprint of Steck-Vaughn Company.

Copyright © 2001 Turnstone Publishing Group, Inc.
Copyright © 2001, text, by Patricia Barnes-Svarney.

Barnes-Svarney, Patricia.
    Secrets of the sun: a closer look at our star/Patricia Barnes-Svarney.
       p. cm. — (Turnstone space explorer)
    Includes bibliographical references and index.
    Summary: Examines the processes and features of the sun, including solar eclipses, sunspot
cycles, coronal mass ejections, and solar wind. Also discusses scientific models and technology
used to study the sun.
    ISBN 0-7398-2214-4 (hardcover) ISBN 0-7398-2224-1 (softcover)

Library of Congress Cataloging-in-Publication Data are available.

For information about this and other Turnstone reference books and educational materials, visit
Turnstone Publishing Group on the World Wide Web at http://www.turnstonepub.com.

Photo and illustration credits listed on page 64 constitute part of this copyright page.

Printed and bound in the United States of America.

1 2 3 4 5 6 7 8 9 0 **LB** 05 04 03 02 01 00

CONTENTS

DISAPPEARING ACT

"There is such a sense of anticipation before an eclipse. And when it occurs, it seems as if you can see the sun's outer atmosphere stretching out to infinity in the sky."—Shadia Habbal

August 11, 1999, was a hot day in Ayn Diwar, on the northeastern tip of Syria. Shadia Habbal, a scientist at the Harvard-Smithsonian Center for Astrophysics (CfA) in Cambridge, Massachusetts, joined others to take pictures of the sun during a total solar eclipse.

Scientists like Shadia spend their lives observing the star closest to Earth, the sun. Some may use photographs for their research. Others may send rockets into the sky. Or they may use an amazing variety of instruments both on Earth and in space to gather data, or information. Scientists study the sun to learn more about its structure, from its center to its surface. They study the sun to learn more about how it creates its light, how it changes with time, and how it releases electrically charged particles from its surface. In this book we talk mostly about the outer parts of the sun.

Shadia has traveled to Syria to view a total solar eclipse. In a total solar eclipse, our moon moves between Earth and the sun. For a brief time, the moon blocks the sun's light that would otherwise reach Earth. During that time, the moon casts a shadow across part of Earth's surface. "Ready... set... there it is!" says Shadia. She snaps her camera as the moon's shadow falls over Ayn Diwar.

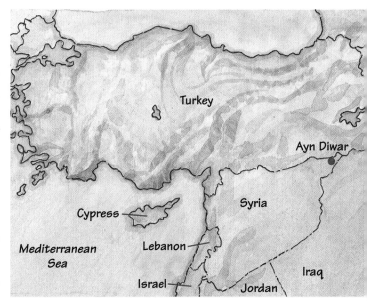

(above)
Some people travel all over the world to see an eclipse. These people are called eclipse chasers. For the solar eclipse on August 11, 1999, many people traveled to Ayn Diwar.

(left)
Here is a photo of the total solar eclipse on February 26, 1998. The bright ring of light is called the sun's corona, or the sun's outer atmosphere.

Preparations to view an eclipse start in the lab, where the scientists gather the equipment they'll need.

Everything happens quickly during a total eclipse. The moon covers the sun completely for only a few minutes. Scientists call this time totality. It's a small window of opportunity for the scientists who want to study the sun during an eclipse. "We really had no time to think," says Shadia. "We had only two minutes and four seconds of totality to take photos. We were completely focused on our experiments."

Shadia studies the sun's corona. The corona is the outer atmosphere of the sun. The light that we see as the sun's "surface" is called the photosphere. It is so bright we can't see the much fainter light that comes from the corona. In fact, it's important to remember not to look directly at the sun. Light from the photosphere can blind you. But during totality, the moon blocks the light from the photosphere. When the photosphere's light is blocked, it becomes possible to see the sun's corona.

During totality, Shadia was busy with her experiments, but she still noticed what happened around her. As the moon moved in front of the sun, the air became a little cooler. The sky turned gray. She could see a few bright stars and planets. And the birds stopped singing.

There were many other people, including scientists and eclipse chasers, gathered to watch the eclipse in Ayn Diwar. As Shadia snapped her camera, it seemed as if hundreds of other cameras clicked at the same time.

In a few minutes, the sun peeked out from behind the moon. The light became brighter. The air warmed up and the birds sang again. It was time to put away the cameras and other equipment. Totality was over.

Equipment is sometimes set up in an open tent like this one in Guadeloupe, an island in the Caribbean Sea. Here, preparations were being made for the total solar eclipse on February 26, 1998.

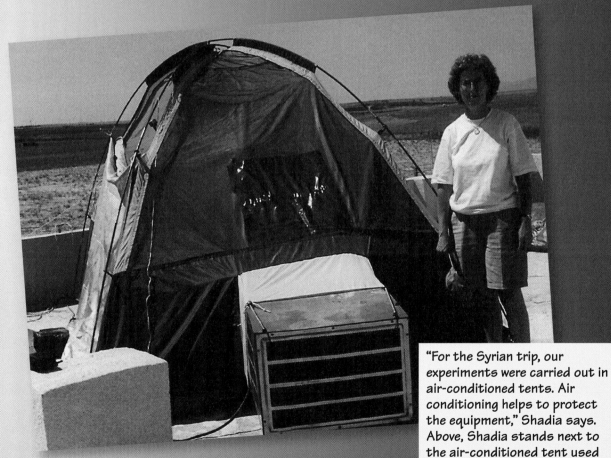

"For the Syrian trip, our experiments were carried out in air-conditioned tents. Air conditioning helps to protect the equipment," Shadia says. Above, Shadia stands next to the air-conditioned tent used for eclipse observations in Ayn Diwar.

Line Up

Total solar eclipses that can be seen from Earth don't happen very often. They take place about once every one to two years. In fact, there were only four total solar eclipses between 1995 and 2000. That's because total solar eclipses happen only when Earth, the moon, and the sun all line up in a certain way.

The moon orbits, or revolves around, Earth once every 29½ days. In one part of its orbit, the moon moves between Earth and the sun. In this position, no sunlight strikes the side of the moon we see from Earth. Without reflected sunlight, we cannot see the side of the moon that faces us. We call this the "new moon."

If the moon moves between Earth and the sun for a part of each orbit, why don't we see a total solar eclipse every month? It's because Earth and the moon move in different planes. A plane is a surface, like a pane of very thin glass. The plane stretches out in all directions.

The moon's orbital plane tilts away from Earth's orbital plane. If the moon were visible as it passed between Earth and the sun, it would most often appear in the sky just above or below the sun. There wouldn't be a total solar eclipse.

The moon's and Earth's orbital planes meet along a line. Occasionally, the moon is on that line when it passes between Earth and the sun. At these times, the sun, moon, and Earth line up almost perfectly. These moments can produce total solar eclipses.

During a total solar eclipse, the moon casts its shadow on a part of Earth's surface called the eclipse path. This path is only about 200 to 300 kilometers (about 125 to 200 miles) wide. The eclipse path seems to move rapidly across Earth's surface. But it is Earth's rotation that creates the appearance of a fast-moving eclipse path.

Below is an eclipse path map made in 1715 by Edmund Halley, for whom Halley's comet is named.

The Right Factors

Because the sun, moon, and Earth move constantly, all three objects must be in certain positions for a solar eclipse to occur. Here are some factors that determine whether conditions are right for a solar eclipse. Note that the objects in these diagrams are not drawn to scale. For example, Earth would appear as a very small dot in the diagram at right if it had been drawn to the same scale as the sun.

❶ Earth's Orbital Plane

Earth moves around the sun in a plane. This diagram shows Earth's orbital plane as if it were seen from above the plane.

Earth

Earth's orbit

Sun

❷ Earth's Tilted Axis

This diagram shows Earth's orbital plane at eye-level, so it looks like a straight line. Earth also rotates around an imaginary axis through its center. Instead of being upright, or perpendicular to the plane of Earth's orbit, Earth's axis is tilted 23.5° from the perpendicular position.

The tilt of Earth's axis affects where day falls on the planet. The eclipse can only be viewed on the daytime side of the planet. The daytime side is the side facing the sun. The moon must pass between Earth and the sun for the eclipse to occur.

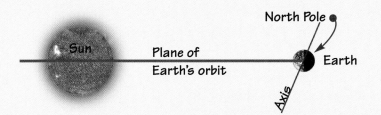

Sun

Plane of
Earth's orbit

North Pole

Earth

Axis

❸ Moon's Orbital Plane

As Earth orbits the sun, the moon orbits Earth. The moon's orbital plane is slanted about 5° from Earth's orbital plane. If the plane were not slanted, there would be an eclipse every month when the moon passes between Earth and the sun.

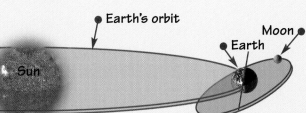

Earth's orbit

Moon

Earth

Sun

Moon's orbit

Note: Objects and orbits are not drawn to scale. In fact, the diameter of Earth's orbit is about 200 times the diameter of the sun, 25,000 times the diameter of Earth, and 100,000 times the diameter of the moon.

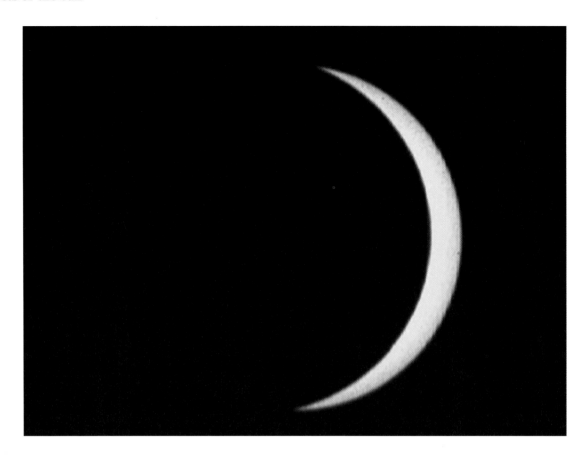

This picture shows the August 11, 1999, solar eclipse. The picture was taken in the country of Croatia, a place to the south of the eclipse path. For that reason, the picture shows a partial eclipse, rather than a total eclipse.
The partial eclipse lasted three hours, and the sun was never completely covered.

To see a total solar eclipse, you must be inside the eclipse path. Beyond that path, only a partial eclipse is visible, at most. Far away, an eclipse can't be seen at all.

In the area where a partial eclipse can be viewed, Earth, the moon, and the sun line up closely, but not perfectly. The moon does not block light from the photosphere completely, making the sun look like someone has taken a bite out of it. Partial eclipses are visible about 3,000 kilometers (about 2,000 miles) on either side of the total eclipse path.

Some scientists, like Shadia, study the sun's corona. This faint outer region can only be seen from Earth's surface if light from the photosphere is blocked. So Shadia and others wait for total solar eclipses. But even when they occur, there is no guarantee that scientists will be able to make the observations they need. At least three conditions are needed.

First, the path of the total eclipse must pass over dry land. Because Earth's surface is mostly water, many eclipse paths fall over oceans. An eclipse with a path over water can be very difficult to study. It's hard to make accurate measurements from the deck of a rocking ship.

Second, conditions at the observing site must be right. If clouds or bad weather block a view of the eclipse, the observations can't be made. "When we traveled to Mongolia for an eclipse, it started to snow a few hours before the eclipse. There was no second chance," says Shadia.

Third, the observation equipment has to work properly. "It is so frustrating if it's cloudy or the equipment breaks down," says Shadia.

Scientists have calculated eclipse paths for many years to come. Below is a map of the eclipse paths for total solar eclipses from 1996 to 2020.

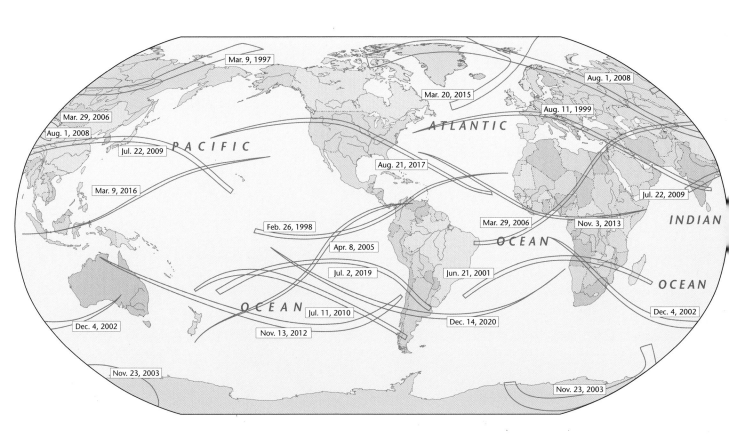

Picturing an Eclipse

These are photographs of the total solar eclipse on August 11, 1999. The eclipse path was about 80 kilometers (about 50 miles) wide. The path stretched from the western Atlantic Ocean through Europe, Turkey, and all the way across India into the Indian Ocean. These photographs were taken in visible light at Lake Hazar, Turkey.

These nine photographs show the stages of the eclipse. To make this sequence, one image was taken every 13.3 minutes. In the far left photograph, the eclipse is just beginning. In the middle photograph, the moon is completely blocking the surface of the sun. In the far right photograph, the eclipse is just about over.

This photo shows small spots of light called Baily's Beads. Baily's Beads occur when the sun's light shines through dips in the moon's bumpy surface. Bailey's Beads can be seen for a few seconds just before and just after totality.

OUR STAR, THE SUN

2

"The Sun, with all the planets revolving around it, and depending on it, can still ripen a bunch of grapes as though it had nothing else in the Universe to do."—Galileo Galilei

The sun is a star, like the ones we can see in the night sky. It is five billion years old. The sun's size, brightness, and mass, or the amount of material in the sun, are average for a star in our galaxy. There are millions of stars that are bigger and brighter than the sun and millions of stars that are smaller and fainter. The sun looks much bigger and brighter to us than other stars do because it is the closest star to Earth.

The sun is the largest object in our solar system. A million Earths could fit inside it. All the planets in our solar system orbit the sun. The planets move in orbits of different diameters.

The sun, like most stars, is a hot, dense collection of mostly hydrogen atoms. A hydrogen atom is the smallest unit of hydrogen. It consists of one proton and one electron. Protons and electrons are oppositely charged particles. They are the smallest charged particles that can travel freely in space. At the sun's core, the temperature is high and the pressure is great. The pressure squeezes the nuclei, or central parts, of the hydrogen atoms. Groups of several protons fuse, or join together. This process is called fusion. During fusion, hydrogen atoms fuse to make helium atoms.

With fusion, huge amounts of energy are released. The sun fuses 600 million metric tons (about 650 million standard tons) of hydrogen into helium each second. There is enough hydrogen at the sun's center to continue fusing this way for about another five billion years.

(above)
Ancient Greeks thought the sun was controlled by a god they called Apollo. They believed that each day, Apollo drove a chariot, pulled by winged horses, across the sky, as is shown on this cup from the 4th century B.C.

(left)
Stonehenge, in England, is a prehistoric monument. It shows that people who lived thousands of years ago were interested in the sun. The arrangement of the remaining stones suggests that the stones were used to tell the first day of summer.

A Closer Look at Our Star

At right is an artist's drawing that shows different regions of the sun. The artist has "cut away" part of the sun's outside regions so that some regions below the surface can be seen.

Core

The core starts at the sun's center and extends in all directions for about 175,000 kilometers (about 110,000 miles). With temperatures higher than 15 million° C (nearly 27 million° F), the core is the hottest part of the sun. It is also very dense. (Density is the amount of matter in a certain quantity of space.) The sun's core is more than 100 times denser than water.

Photosphere

The sun is a giant ball without a solid surface. The sun's "surface" is just the uppermost layer, which is dense enough that an observer on Earth cannot see through it. The photosphere is about 300 to 400 kilometers (about 200 to 250 miles) thick, with a temperature of about 5,800° C (about 10,000° F).

Sunspots

Sunspots are dark, irregular spots on the photosphere. They constantly change their shapes and positions. A sunspot lasts from less than one hour to up to six months. The average sunspot is about as large as Earth. A sunspot's typical surface temperature is about 4,000° C (7,000° F).

Chromosphere

This region extends about 10,000 kilometers (about 6,200 miles) above the photosphere. Temperatures average 7,500° C (about 13,500° F).

Corona

The corona is the outermost region of the sun. It extends far into space and is the only part of the sun that can be seen during a total solar eclipse. The corona is much hotter than the photosphere, reaching several million degrees C. It is made of charged particles, mainly protons and electrons.

Corona

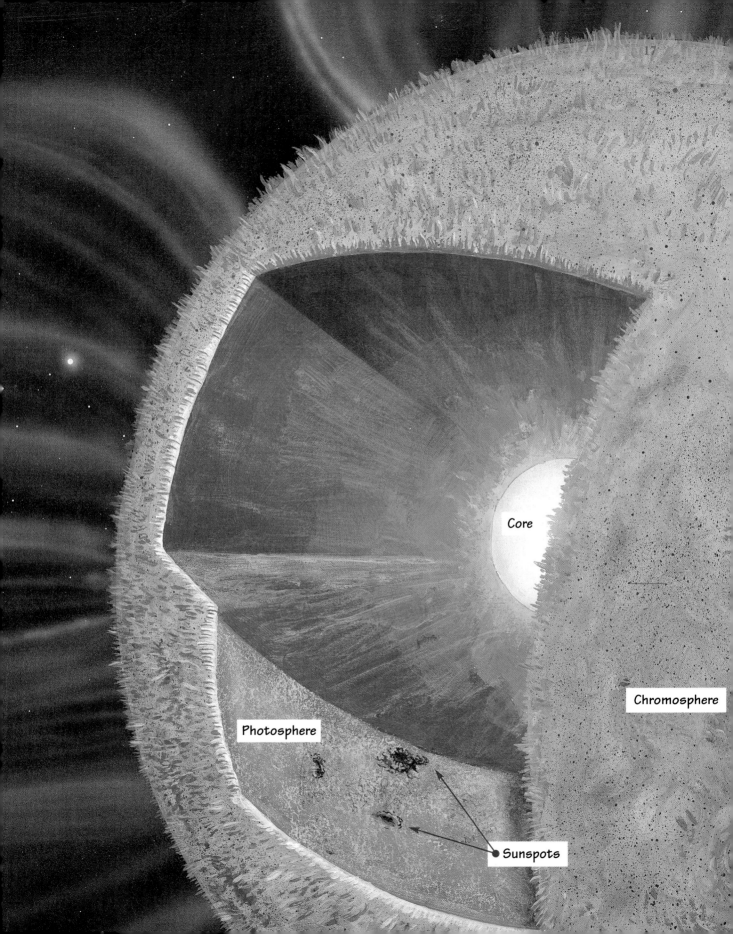

Modeling the Behavior of Light

To study stars like the sun, scientists need a model of how light behaves and how it moves. Light is very mysterious. The more scientists study it, the more mysterious it seems. But some of its properties, or characteristics, can be modeled fairly simply. Models allow scientists to predict light's behavior.

One characteristic of light is how it moves from place to place. Light seems to travel in straight lines. To describe this behavior, scientists model light as rays.

Some of light's behavior cannot be described by rays. It is better described using a wave model. In this model, light is represented by waves. Their lengths can be from near zero to near infinity. Different objects and processes in nature give off different amounts of light at the various wavelengths.

The light we see is called visible light. Visible light has a range of colors. Each color is represented by a certain wavelength, or range of wavelengths. In a rainbow, light is separated into a spectrum, or series of colors. They appear in this order—red, orange, yellow, green, blue, indigo, and violet. In the wave model, wavelengths of light become shorter in this same order. Red light has the longest wavelength, and violet has the shortest wavelength. The chart below shows the names that are used for different wavelengths of light. Light with the shortest wavelengths is called gamma rays. Light with the longest wavelengths is called radio waves.

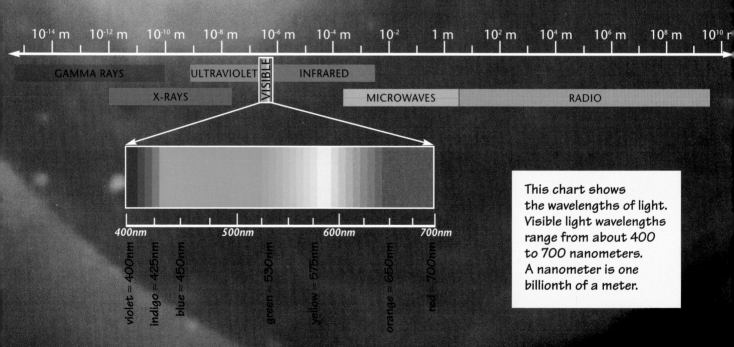

This chart shows the wavelengths of light. Visible light wavelengths range from about 400 to 700 nanometers. A nanometer is one billionth of a meter.

Sun Pictures

Shadia and other solar scientists use filters on their cameras to make images of the sun. These filters are special glass lenses. The filters allow only certain ranges of wavelengths, or certain colors, to pass through them. These filters allow the scientists to choose what range of light they want to use for their pictures.

"In all of astronomy, you learn so much without touching anything, just from the light you're getting," says Shadia. "It's through the light that you're able to make all these discoveries. To me, this is the most fascinating thing."

This picture of the photosphere was made by a scientist using a filter that blocked all colors but orange. That is why the photosphere looks orange in this picture. Shadia uses a similar filter when she takes pictures of the corona.

This picture, also of the photosphere, was made by a scientist using a different filter. This filter blocked all colors but red.

Coronagraphs

Because scientists didn't want to wait for infrequent solar eclipses to study the sun, they invented a device called a coronagraph. A coronagraph can be attached to an Earth-based telescope, or to a spacecraft in orbit. When a coronagraph is aimed at the sun, the device's dark disk works like the moon during an eclipse. The disk blocks the photosphere's light. So, by masking the photosphere, a coronagraph makes it possible to photograph most of the corona.

Some coronagraphs are attached to telescopes high on mountaintops, where they are less affected by Earth's atmosphere. Other coronagraphs are attached to spacecraft that orbit above Earth's atmosphere. From there, they can photograph the corona very clearly.

Shadia and other scientists often use coronagraphs to study the outer parts of the sun's corona. Then why do scientists still travel all over the world to photograph total solar eclipses? Because coronagraphs are not perfect. For example, Earth's atmosphere scatters sunlight that travels through it. This scattered light enters Earth-based telescopes and makes pictures of the corona fuzzier. Also, using coronagraphs aboard satellites is much more expensive than photographing a natural eclipse from Earth.

The Mauna Loa Solar Observatory is located on the Mauna Loa volcano on the island of Hawaii. This observatory has five specialized instruments that scientists use to make observations of the sun.

Scientists observe the sun because they want to learn about the behavior of its different parts. Observations help scientists create models, or theories, of how the sun and other stars work. Models are the means that scientists have to predict nature's behavior.

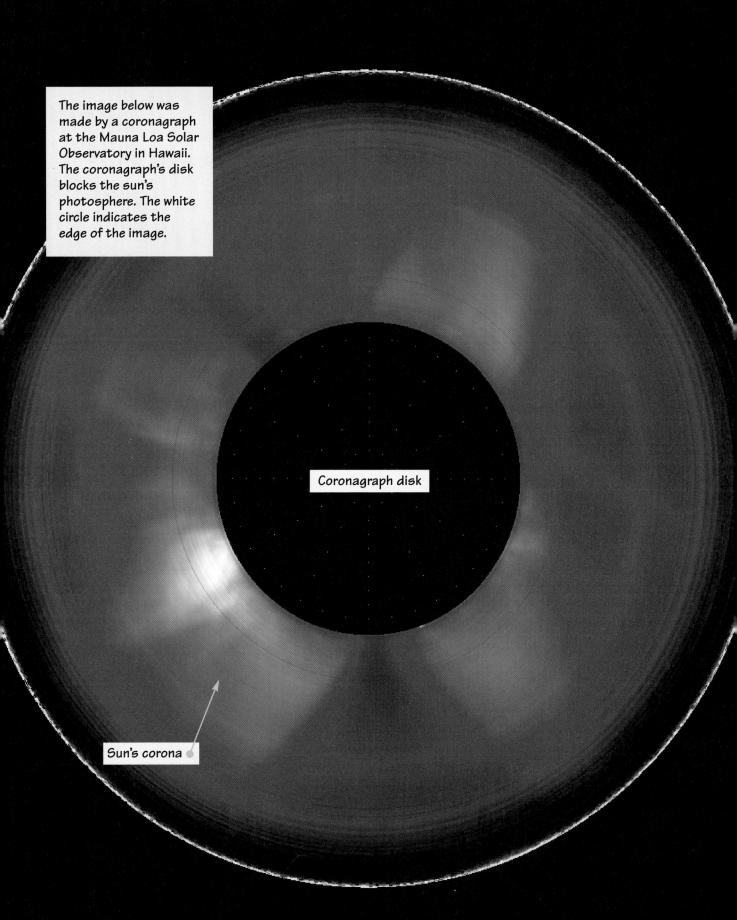

The image below was made by a coronagraph at the Mauna Loa Solar Observatory in Hawaii. The coronagraph's disk blocks the sun's photosphere. The white circle indicates the edge of the image.

Coronagraph disk

Sun's corona

CAPTURING THE CROWN

"Events from the sun that blow past Earth cause very dramatic effects above our atmosphere and sometimes even down to ground level."—Leon Golub

Some of the light that comes from the sun is harmful to us. X-ray light is one example. Earth's atmosphere absorbs this light and keeps it from reaching the ground. But X-rays can tell scientists something about what's going on above the sun's photosphere.

One scientist interested in studying X-rays from the sun is CfA scientist Leon Golub. Leon and fellow scientists launch rockets from the White Sands Missile Range in New Mexico. Leon's rockets don't orbit Earth. Instead, they rise up about 300 kilometers (about 200 miles), taking photographs along the way. Then the rocket falls back to Earth. The whole trip takes about five minutes. "Rockets are cheap and quick to build," says Leon. "We try to reuse them, but sometimes the rocket breaks apart, especially if it hits a rock as it lands."

Each rocket carries a special telescope that can collect X-ray light. The telescope is in a section of the rocket that is about half a meter (nearly two feet) wide and about two meters (nearly seven feet) long.

The telescope collects light that shows what the sun would look like if we could see it with "X-ray eyes." Leon is particularly interested in seeing the sun's corona.

(above)
Leon uses this Terrier Black Brant rocket to take X-ray images.

(left)
This image of the sun was made during one of the rocket flights. The mark across the image's top is a scratch on the film. It happened when the rocket's parachute didn't open correctly and the rocket crashed. The film fell out and was exposed to light.

X-ray Eyes

Not all parts of the corona are the same. "There are places where the corona is bright," Leon says. "There are places where it's faint. There are places where it's hotter than average. There are places where it's cooler." Leon and other scientists are trying to develop a model to predict the corona's behavior.

Although one part of the corona may be quite different from another, all the corona's parts are still extremely hot. The charged particles that make up the corona have extremely high speeds and move in all different directions. The temperatures of these charged particles can be greater than 2,000,000° C (nearly 4,000,000° F). At such very high temperatures, X-rays can be produced.

The telescope inside each rocket has a thin metal filter in front of it. This filter blocks visible light given off by the sun's photosphere. But it allows X-rays to enter the telescope. The telescope takes pictures of the sun at several different wavelengths of X-ray light. Leon and other scientists study the pictures and try to determine the temperature of the charged particles in different parts of the corona. The pictures help scientists learn more about the sun's entire corona.

"The problem with a rocket is that it's only up there for about five minutes," Leon says. "It's not up long enough to really see how things change." Also, Leon only launches a rocket about once a year.

To get more information about the sun, Leon uses other pictures taken in space. He now uses data collected

Leon Golub and other scientists use observations made in X-ray light to study the sun's corona. These scientists are working to create a model that correctly predicts the corona's behavior.

Capturing a Corona

This image was made by combining two separate images. They were taken at the same moment from two different locations. An X-ray image from one of Leon's rockets was added to a visible-light image taken during a total eclipse. The X-ray image from the rocket shows the sun's photosphere. The image taken during the eclipse shows visible light from the sun's corona. During a total solar eclipse, the sun's photosphere is blocked. Then it's possible for scientists to take images of the corona from Earth.

In the picture below, the X-ray image has been placed on top of the eclipse image. By putting images together this way, scientists can gain much more complete pictures of the corona.

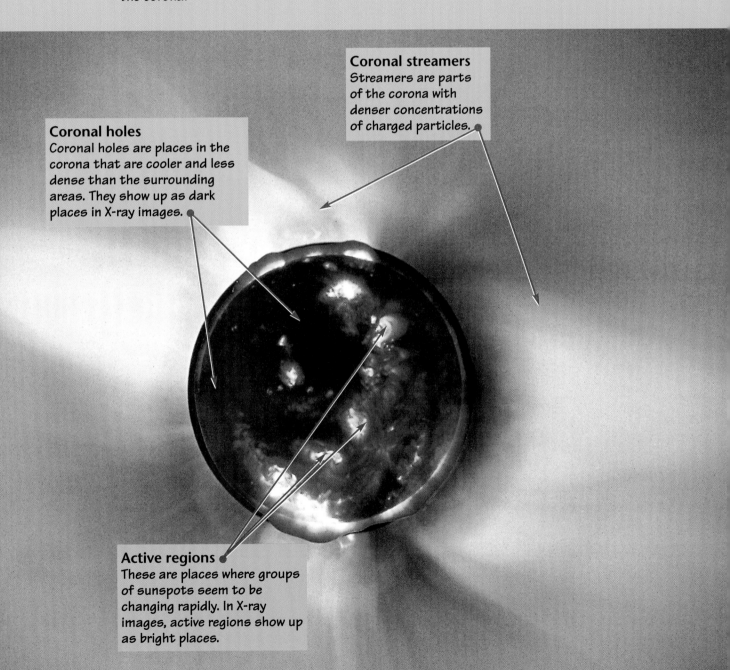

Coronal streamers
Streamers are parts of the corona with denser concentrations of charged particles.

Coronal holes
Coronal holes are places in the corona that are cooler and less dense than the surrounding areas. They show up as dark places in X-ray images.

Active regions
These are places where groups of sunspots seem to be changing rapidly. In X-ray images, active regions show up as bright places.

by a satellite that was launched in 1998. It's called the Transition Region and Coronal Explorer (TRACE). TRACE orbits in a path that lets it observe the sun without interruption for up to eight months at a time. The satellite helps Leon and other scientists track how the surface of the sun and its corona change over periods of time up to several years.

Instruments on TRACE, shown at right, have filters and specially coated mirrors. These instruments collect light from different regions of the corona. By studying the light, scientists can better describe the corona.

Three colored images were combined to make this TRACE image of part of the sun's corona. One image is colored blue, another green, and the other red. Red represents the longest, and blue the shortest, wavelengths of visible light given off by the sun's corona.

This picture of the corona was made during the total solar eclipse of August 11, 1999. It is a combination of many images, specially treated to bring out faint features. Pictures like these help scientists see details of the corona's features.

Heating Up

Leon also studies coronas in other stars like the sun. Coronas seem to be common in these stars. But the coronas of different stars may be different in several ways. "Younger stars give off more X-ray light," Leon notes. Scientists are trying to figure out if the sun's corona also gave off more X-ray light when the sun was younger. If so, billions of years ago Earth could have been bathed in an intense stream of solar X-rays. "It's even possible that the corona of the sun, when the sun was younger, might have determined if life formed on this planet," Leon says. The X-rays might have prevented life from forming during that time. It's also possible that changes in X-ray intensity could have caused changes in the atmosphere that allowed life to form.

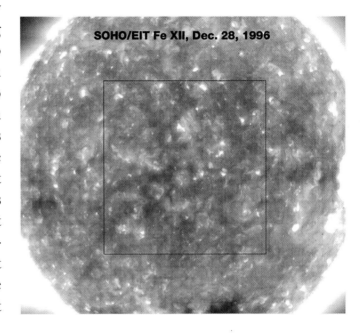

This image was made by the Solar and Heliospheric Observatory's (SOHO) Extreme-ultraviolet Imaging Telescope (EIT). The rectangle within the image encloses a part that will be the site of a detailed study of microflares. Images like these are colored to make it easier for scientists to see details.

Scientists continue to make observations of the corona as they try to improve their model of how it behaves. For example, scientists still have no model for the corona's high temperature. "That is still a mystery," Leon says. "It's not something we would have predicted." Scientists would expect temperatures to get cooler farther away from the surface of the sun. Instead, the corona gets hotter farther away from the sun's surface. "This is a very strange thing," Leon says.

Recent observations made using TRACE may hold the key. TRACE findings show a nearly steady series of tiny explosions called microflares in lower parts of the corona. These microflares may help heat the rest of the corona. "There's still a lot to learn," Leon says. "But we're making progress."

Seeing Double

It can be useful for scientists to compare the sun in different kinds of light. Here are two pictures of the sun made on the same day by the Yohkoh Observatory. Yohkoh is a satellite launched from Kogshima, Japan, on August 31, 1991. The picture of the sun on this page was made in visible light. The picture of the sun on the next page was made in X-ray light.

By studying the sun in both X-ray and visible light, scientists have observed that the positions of the active regions in the sun's corona seem to be near sunspot locations in the sun's photosphere.

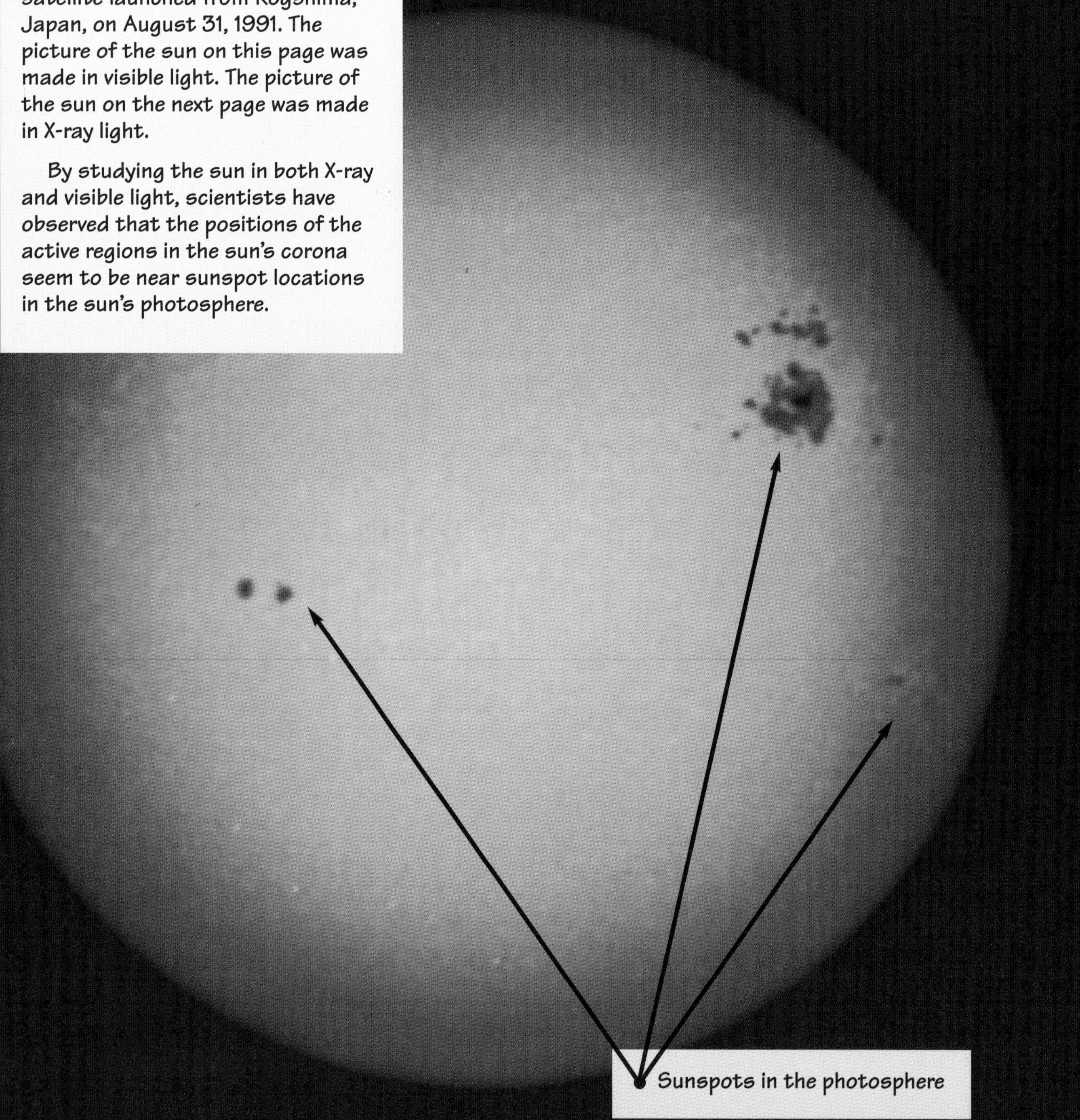

Visible light image

Sunspots in the photosphere

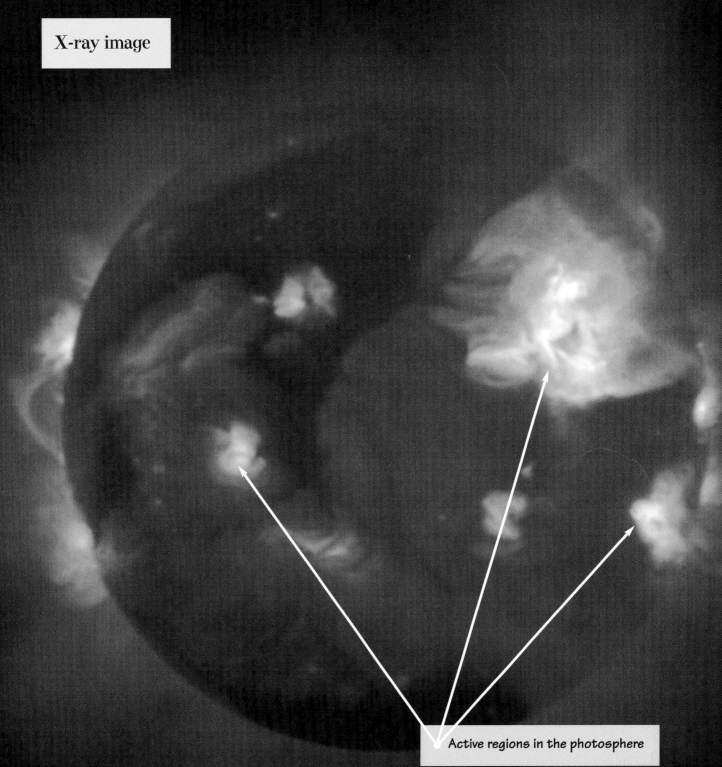

X-ray image

Active regions in the photosphere

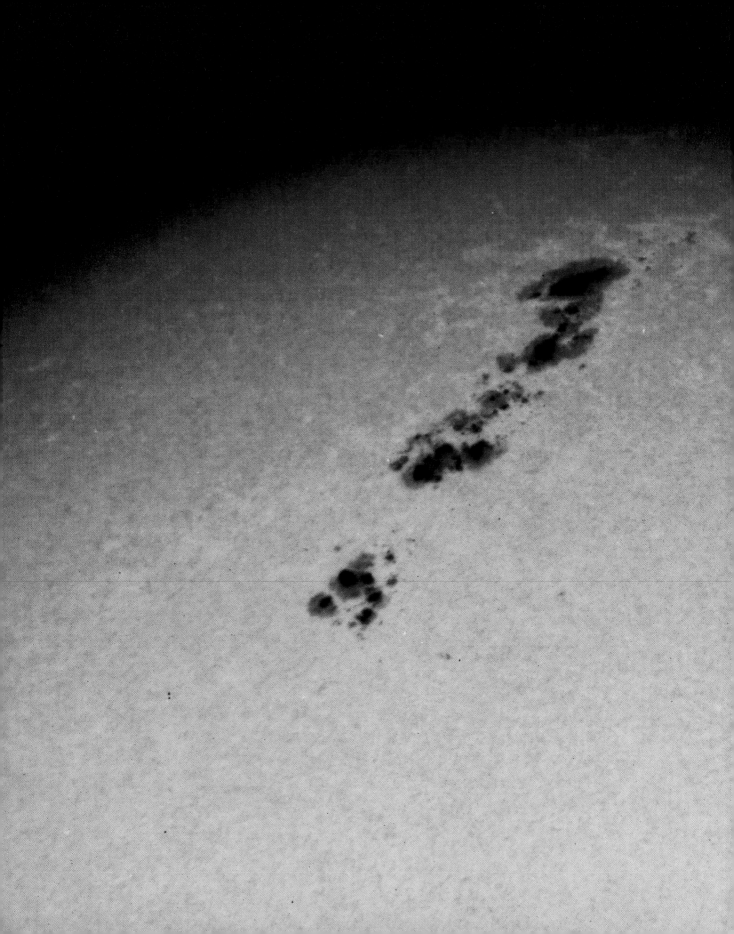

4
SPOTS ON THE SUN

"Sunspots last from a few days to weeks. They make the sun's face look as if it has freckles."—Sallie Baliunas

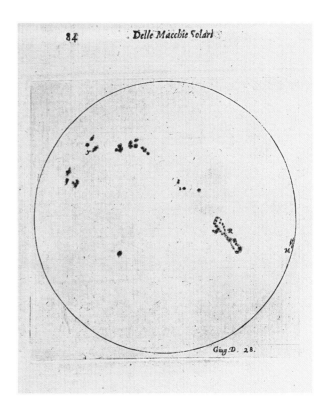

The invention of the telescope in 1607 made more detailed observation of the sky possible. Italian scientist Galileo Galilei (1564 –1642) was one of the first people to observe the sun through a telescope. In 1610, Galileo observed sunspots. Sunspots are dark, irregular spots on the sun's surface. Galileo noticed that sunspots moved over time. He thought the spots moved because the sun rotated. Over the centuries since Galileo's observations, many scientists have studied sunspots. Scientists also have observed that a sunspot's lifetime can range from less than one hour to up to six months.

One scientist who is interested in sunspots is Sallie Baliunas. Sallie works at the CfA. She has studied sunspots for more than 20 years. Sallie describes sunspots as places where the sun's magnetic field "pops" above the sun's surface. "It's almost as if the sun's magnetic field wants to 'float' on top of the sun," she says.

(above)
Galileo drew pictures to record the positions of the sunspots. This drawing is from his book *Letters on Sunspots*, published in 1613.

(left)
Some sunspots, such as these, have a dark center and a lighter ring around the outside.

Magnets and Models

If you hold the ends of two bar magnets together, you will feel either a force pushing them apart or a force pulling them together. Each bar magnet has two ends, called "north" and "south" poles. Two poles of the same type push each other away. And two poles that are of opposite types attract one another.

When you sprinkle iron filings near a bar magnet, the filings line up in a pattern like the one shown at right. When scientists make a model of this behavior, they draw lines that arch between the poles of the magnet. Scientists call these lines magnetic field lines.

Because Earth and the sun are somewhat like bar magnets, they have magnetic field lines that arch between their poles. And the properties of their magnetic fields change over time. The sun's overall magnetic field is not as strong as Earth's. The surface of the sun, however, exhibits powerful magnetic activity, while Earth's surface does not. The overall bar-magnet property of the sun's magnetic field may change up to 100,000 times more rapidly than the bar-magnet property of Earth's magnetic field.

To understand how sunspots behave, scientists rely on their models of how magnets work. According to scientists' models, sunspots come in pairs. Each sunspot in a pair acts like one pole of a magnet. A magnetic field arches between these poles.

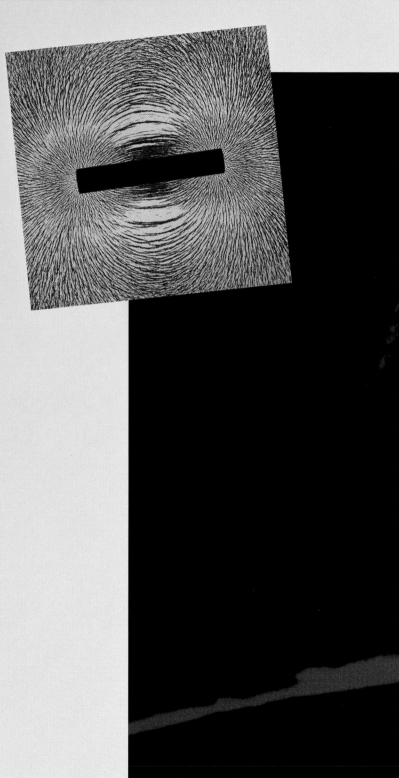

The photo below shows a solar prominence, or a cloud of electrically charged particles. These charged particles give off light as they arch between two sunspots. Solar prominences trace the magnetic field lines between the sunspots in a sunspot pair. Solar prominences make the magnetic field lines between sunspot pairs visible to observers on Earth.

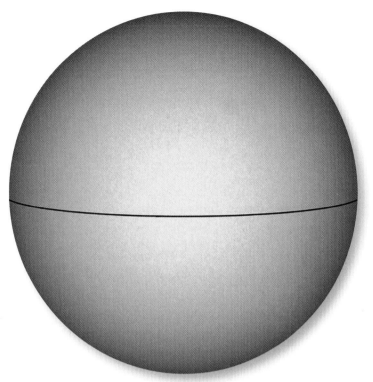

January 4, 1994

These images of the sun were taken during an 11-year sunspot cycle. They show a change from a time of almost no sunspots in 1994 to many sunspots in 2000.

The Sunspot Cycle

The average number of sunspots that scientists can observe on the sun's surface changes in a nearly predictable way. Each such pattern of changes in the number of sunspots is called a sunspot cycle. A sunspot cycle lasts about 11 years.

When the cycle begins, few sunspots are visible. As the years pass, the number of visible sunspots slowly increases. Toward the peak of the cycle, as many as 300 sunspots may be seen from Earth at one time. Then, the number of sunspots begins to decrease. The number of sunspots slowly drops almost to zero until the cycle begins again.

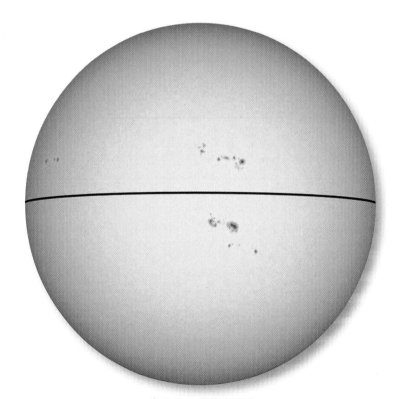

October 30, 1996

"A sunspot doesn't look like very much in a photograph," says Sallie. "What's exciting about sunspots is watching what happens to them over time—watching their numbers increase, watching the surface of the sun get 'freckled' with hundreds of spots. And then watching them disappear, so that the sun is left almost unspotted at times." Scientists are trying to develop a model of this process to predict the future formation of sunspots.

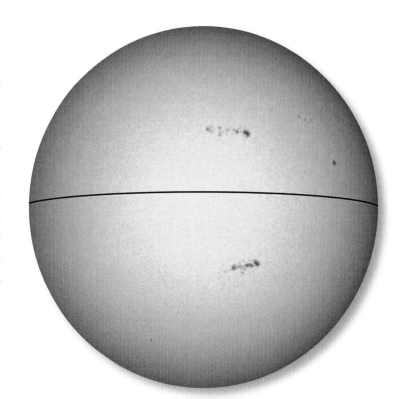

January 19, 1999

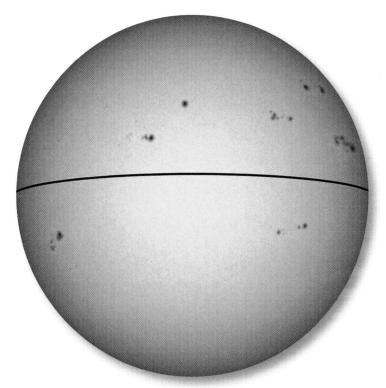

March 22, 2000

Modeling the Sunspot Cycle

Galileo's careful observations of the sun convinced him that sunspots move. He had assumed that sunspots were fixed to the sun's surface. So why did they move? Galileo concluded that their motion shows that the sun rotates. His conclusion has long been accepted. Today scientists still use the movement of sunspots to study the rotation of the sun.

In the 1850s scientists observed that sunspots at different latitudes on the sun seemed to move across the sun's surface at different speeds. The scientists observed that sunspots near the sun's equator needed 25 days to move around the sun. Sunspots halfway between the sun's equator and its poles took a few days longer. And near

These pictures show the movement of sunspots over four days in June 2000. All the pictures were taken at the same time of day. Arrows in each picture indicate the same sunspot groups on different days.

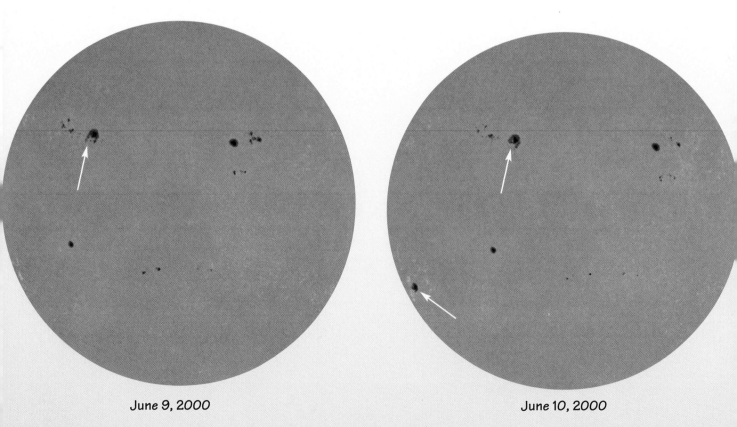

June 9, 2000

June 10, 2000

the sun's poles, sunspots took as long as 35 days to move all the way around the sun. If sunspots are fixed to the sun's surface, these observations show that different parts of the sun's surface rotate at different speeds. Scientists are puzzled by this behavior. The models they have created so far are not good enough to predict these differences in rotation.

Scientists' models of the sunspot cycle are also quite primitive. They leave many questions unanswered. For instance, the models do not address the fact that the cycle occasionally stops. There are times when the sun shows no sunspot activity for decades. Sallie and other scientists want to know how and why there is a sunspot cycle and why it sometimes "pauses."

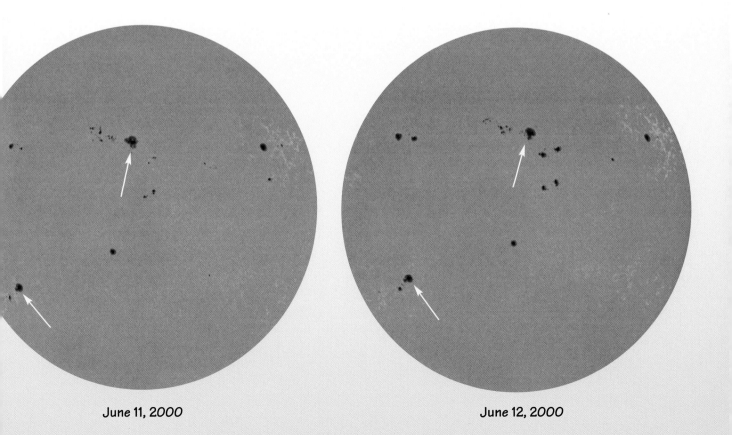

June 11, 2000   June 12, 2000

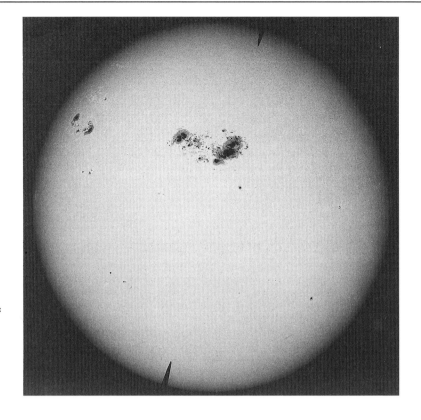

This 1947 photograph shows one of the largest sunspot groups ever recorded. It stretched for about 300,000 kilometers (about 200,000 miles), almost the distance from Earth to the moon.

The Maunder Minimum

Between the years 1645 and 1715, scientists saw almost no sunspots on the surface of the sun. This period of time is called the Maunder Minimum. During the Maunder Minimum, northern Europe experienced unusually cold winters. The rivers froze. Huge, thick sheets of ice called glaciers inched down mountain slopes and through valleys.

Were the unusually cold temperatures on Earth connected to a lack of sunspots? "We really don't know," Sallie Baliunas says. "But we think the 11-year cycle is too short to affect the climate in any major way." What about the effects on climate of a long pause in the sunspot cycle? No one knows for sure what they are.

Changes on the sun can take from seconds to billions of years. Have any of these changes affected life and the environment on Earth? "That's a question I have studied and will continue to study," says Sallie.

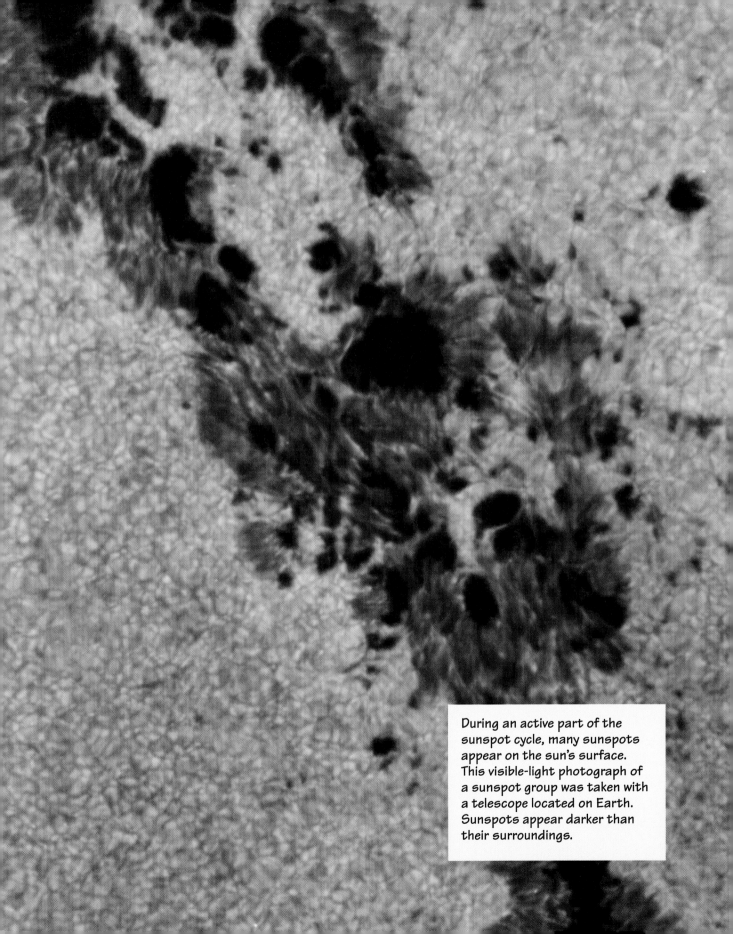

During an active part of the sunspot cycle, many sunspots appear on the sun's surface. This visible-light photograph of a sunspot group was taken with a telescope located on Earth. Sunspots appear darker than their surroundings.

Sallie is standing at the base of Mount Wilson Observatory near Pasadena, California (bottom). Sallie uses a device attached to the telescope to make measurements of stars that are at different stages of their lives.

Seeing Spots

Sallie tries to learn more about sunspots by studying other stars. Sunspots are visible on the sun because the sun is the closest star to Earth. Other stars are much too far away to see directly any spots they might have. Sallie says, "I have to 'see' spots on other stars by some other method." Though Sallie can't see these "starspots," she can find signs that they exist.

Based on observations of the sun, there may be a direct connection between the number of starspots and the amount of light given off by calcium atoms in the star. The greater the amount of calcium detected, the more starspots there may be.

So, Sallie looks carefully for evidence of calcium in the light from other stars. She concludes, "In stars where calcium light glows more strongly, there may be more spots." By tracking the brightness of light given off by calcium atoms in a star, Sallie hopes she will be following starspot cycles.

In this way Sallie has found evidence that other sun-like stars have starspot cycles that are similar to the sun's cycle. She has observed that younger stars tend to have less regular cycles. Their starspots also give off more light from calcium atoms.

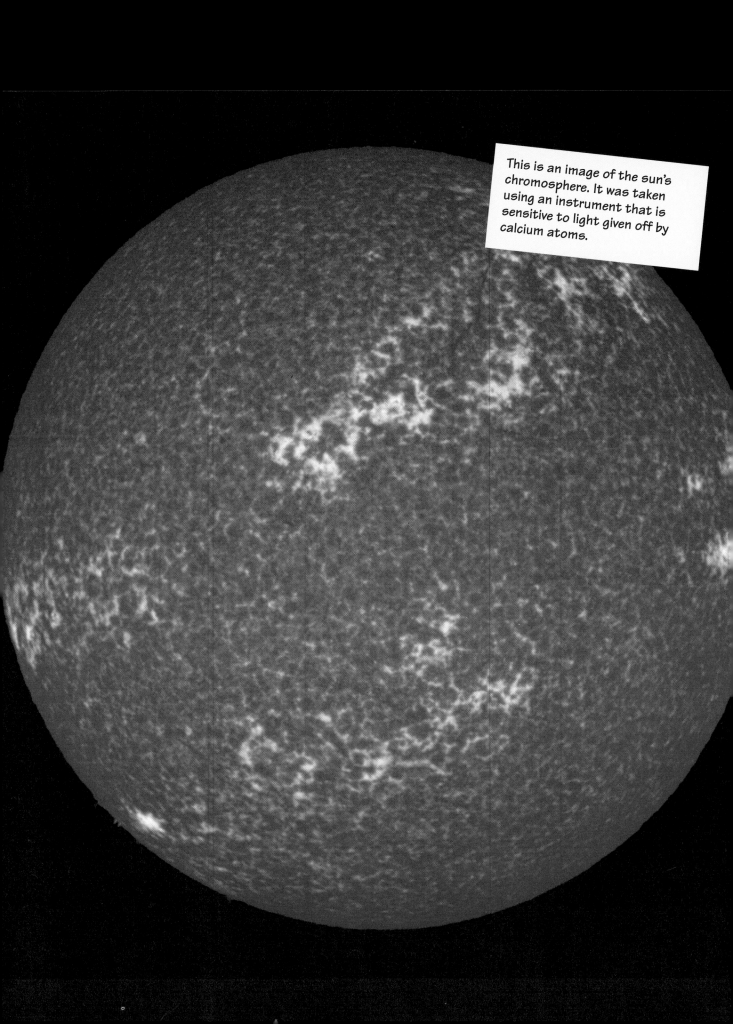

This is an image of the sun's chromosphere. It was taken using an instrument that is sensitive to light given off by calcium atoms.

Galileo contributed greatly to the fields of mathematics and physics, as well as astronomy.

Predictions

The sun's predicted 10-billion-year lifetime is much longer than that of any individual scientist. Therefore, to study the behavior of the sun, scientists continue the observations of scientists who came before them. For example, scientists today are still adding to records of observations started by Galileo in the 1600s.

So how do scientists gather the information they need? One way is to observe stars that are like the sun, as Sallie does. "In our galaxy there are many other stars that are like the sun, but in different stages of their lives.

THE ASTROPHYSICAL JOURNAL, 450:896–901, 1995 September 10
© 1995. The American Astronomical Society. All rights reserved. Printed in U.S.A.

ARE VARIATIONS IN THE LENGTH OF THE ACTIVITY CYCLE RELATED TO CHANGES
IN BRIGHTNESS IN SOLAR-TYPE STARS?

SALLIE BALIUNAS AND WILLIE SOON
Harvard-Smithsonian Center for Astrophysics, 60 Garden Street, Cambridge, MA 02138
Received 1995 February 2; accepted 1995 March 21

ABSTRACT

We compare the average level of chromospheric activity and cycle length for solar-type stars as determined from 25 yr records of Ca II fluxes and from the sunspot record from 1750 to 1990. Both sets of data show an inverse relation between the cycle length and average activity level, with only a minor difference in the slopes. In turn, the amplitude of Ca II variability is positively correlated with the photometric brightness change during an activity cycle. The relationship between those observables provides a physical basis for the close correlation between the length of the sunspot cycle and mean terrestrial temperature over the last few centuries as shown by Friis-Christensen & Lassen. . . . estimated from this relationship by including stars with low Ca II fluxes which, we assume, are in states r . . . . of solar activity known as the Maunder minimum (circa 1645–1715). Although the value . . . . activity and the cycle length is sensitive to the statistical treatm . . . . be determined reliably. This lower limit yields an increase of 0 . . . . minimum to the cyclic phase of sunspot activity which immedi . . . .
Subject headings: stars: activity — stars: chromospheres — sta . . . .
Sun: activity — sunspots

1. INTRODUCTION

In a recent study, Friis-Christensen & Lassen (1991) illustrated a correlation between the sunspot cycle length and changes in both the mean northern hemisphere or global land air temperature over the last century. The close timing between changes in the two quantities adds to the long history of evidence for the effects of solar variability on terrestrial climate change over decades to centuries (e.g., Eddy 1977a; Mitchell, Stockton, & Meko 1979; Wigley & Kelly 1990; Parker 1994). Such short timescale variations are related to near-surface magnetic changes. Those short-term variations are distinct from the variations connected with the thermal relaxation of the entire solar convective zone, which occurs on a timescale ~10⁵ yr (e.g., Gough 1990), or the variations associated with the hypothesized connection between the secular changes in Earth's orbit about the Sun and climate (97, 40, and 21 kyr; Milankovitch 1941).

One possible explanation of the correlation shown by Friis-Christensen & Lassen (1991) is a climatically significant change in solar total irradiance, for which the changes in the length of the sunspot cycle are a proxy (we will not consider other possible mechanisms of changes in climate change, e.g., a hypothetical effect of changes in solar ultraviolet flux which would alter the dynamics of the atmosphere). We examine the possibility of solar total irradiance change linked to change surface magnetic activity by comparing information from observational results of the Sun and solar which are close in mass and age (e.g., Lockwo Zhang et al. 1994; Baliunas et al. 1995).

The underlying premise in comparative and other solar-type stars is stellar equi tistically similar magnetic activity beh similar physical properties. Stellar equ magnetic behavior (and the associa . . .

Galileo published *Letters on Sunspots* in 1613. Sallie published a paper on the sunspot cycle in 1995. Although the format of a scientific research paper has changed over the past 400 years, sunspots remain a subject of interest.

I observe them to put together a picture of the sun's past, present, and future," says Sallie.

In 1966 scientist Olin Wilson began a program at the Mount Wilson Observatory in the San Gabriel Mountains north of Pasadena, California. The purpose of the program was to observe 100 stars like the sun every month, year after year.

Sallie joined the program in 1977. She still spends about one week each month at the observatory. Each night of that week, she observes between 60 and 100 stars. Sallie's findings, and those of other people in the project, are intended to help scientists correctly describe the sun's past and predict its future.

Sallie focuses her research on sunspots. Like many scientists, she has chosen one topic to study in depth.

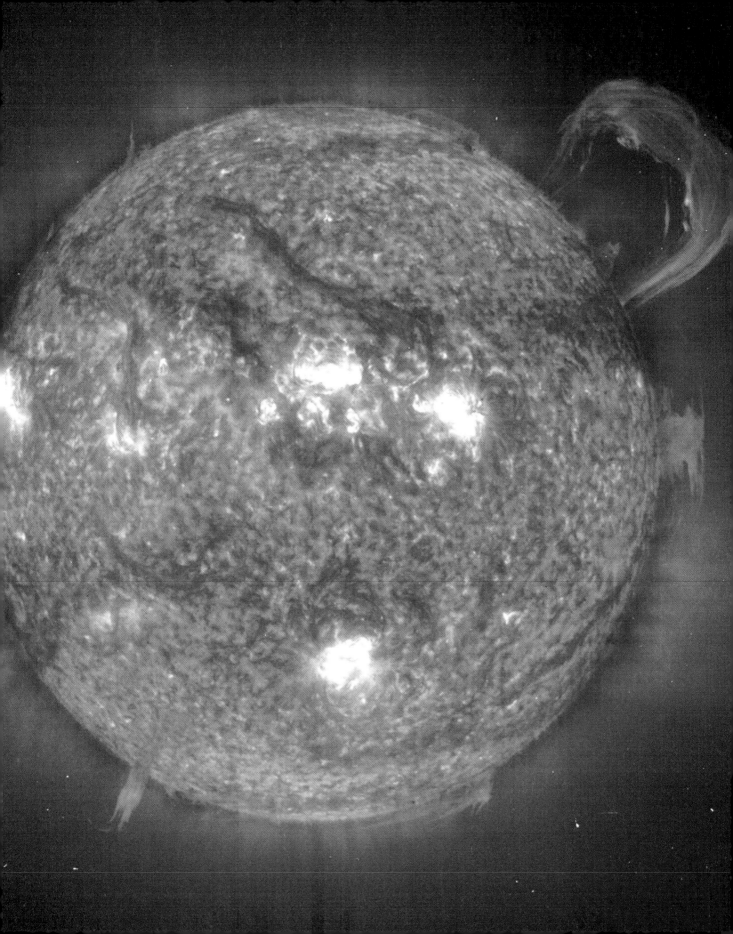

5

FIREWORKS FROM THE SUN

"What makes the sun throw out this tremendous mass of particles in one moment, and send it into space?"—Margarita Karovska

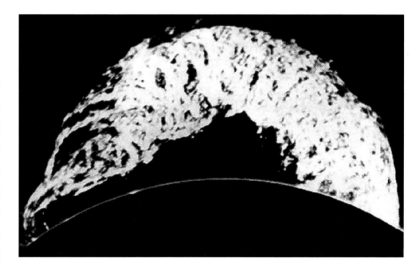

Sunspots are just one example of solar activity. The sun also creates sudden bright spots called solar flares. It can give off huge loops of hot gas called prominences. The sun also has Coronal Mass Ejections (CMEs). CMEs are the largest releases of material from any major body in the solar system. During a CME, the photosphere suddenly releases millions of tons of tiny, hot, electrically charged particles into the corona. From there the particles move into space. If these particles reach Earth, they can cause all kinds of electrical problems.

One scientist who wants to learn more about CMEs is Margarita Karovska from the CfA. "I'm trying to understand CMEs. How do they happen? How does the sun's magnetic field shape them? How do they travel?" Margarita asks.

Margarita studies CMEs by looking at images of the sun taken by an instrument on board the Solar and Heliospheric Observatory (SOHO) spacecraft, a satellite launched in 1995. This instrument is made of three different coronagraphs whose images can be combined.

(above)
In June 1947, this loop of gas, called the Grand Daddy Prominence, reached so high that a planet the size of Earth would fit beneath it.

(left)
This picture of the sun was taken by SOHO on September 23, 1999. A handle-shaped prominence can be seen in the upper right corner of the photograph. In this picture, the hottest areas appear almost white, while cooler areas, such as the prominence, are shown in dark red. These "false colors" are used to show temperature differences.

March 20, 2000, 9:06 A.M.
This is the beginning of a CME.

This is a coronal hole.

This dark region is the part that is blocked by the coronagraph's disk.

March 20, 2000, 9:54 A.M.
The CME is swelling out from the sun's corona.

March 20, 2000, 10:30 A.M.
The CME is moving out from the sun.

March 20, 2000, 11:06 A.M.
The leading edge of the CME is moving farther off into space.

These four pictures were taken by instruments on SOHO. They were taken over a period of two hours on March 20, 2000. The pictures show a CME blast that sent an estimated one billion metric tons of charged particles traveling rapidly into outer space. The white circle in each image marks the edge of the photosphere.

The first of these three coronagraphs is called C1. The C1 coronagraph looks at the corona close to the photosphere. C2 views the corona a little farther from the photosphere. And C3 studies the parts of the corona even farther from the photosphere. Unlike TRACE or Leon's rockets, the coronagraphs that are on SOHO observe visible light.

Another SOHO instrument, the Extreme-ultraviolet Imaging Telescope (EIT), also helps Margarita and other scientists learn more about the sun's corona. The EIT collects ultraviolet light, or light from the sun with wavelengths in the ultraviolet range. When a CME takes place, this telescope shows a quick brightening of a region on the sun's inner corona. The telescope then shows a small loop of material expanding from this spot.

As the loop expands, the C1 coronagraph picks it up. "As it moves farther away, you can see it in the C2 coronagraph. Then you can follow it with C3," Margarita says. She looks for characteristics in the shape of a CME that make the CME different from the region around it. She follows the development of the CME in several pictures. For example, she watches to see how its position and speed change. Observing these changes helps her infer, or make a thoughtful guess about, what makes a CME move from the sun's surface into space.

Margarita Karovska uses SOHO images to track CMEs. "A CME usually appears like a large loop with a dark space below it, pushing outward," Margarita says.

Acting Up

Prominences often erupt together with CMEs. Scientists are working to find out if there is a relationship between these events.

These images taken by SOHO show prominences and CMEs. By studying images such as these, scientists may find clues about when a prominence is going to appear. Knowledge of these clues may give watchers on Earth more warning of a possible CME.

August 26, 1997, prominence

September 14, 1997, prominence

Heading for Earth

The number of CMEs follows the sunspot cycle. When there are many sunspots, there are usually more CMEs, too. When there are fewer sunspots, there are usually fewer CMEs. On an average day, at the peak of solar activity, three or four CMEs may be released. Several times each month, a CME heads straight for our planet.

Although particles from a CME travel at speeds of more than 300 kilometers (about 200 miles) per second, they may take up to six days to reach Earth. When the particles finally arrive, they can interfere with many peoples' lives. In May 1998 a CME may have caused a communications satellite to fail. Millions of people lost telephone-pager service that day.

CME particles can produce electrical currents on Earth. The currents don't affect people's health, but they can possibly damage electrical equipment on the ground.

On March 13, 1989, a powerful CME hit Earth. The CME caused an electrical surge along power lines and in power stations in parts of Quebec, Canada. More than six million people lost electrical

November 28, 1996, CME

EIT image

C2 coronagraph disk

C2 coronagraph image

C3 coronagraph image

power for nearly nine hours in the middle of a very cold winter night. Some people who owned automatic garage-door openers found their garage doors opening and closing all by themselves.

To prepare for problems like these, someone is always watching the sun for CMEs. Researchers at the National Aeronautics and Space Administration's (NASA's) Goddard Space Flight Center in Greenbelt, Maryland, watch images from SOHO's EIT instrument. They look for signs that a CME is occurring. If a CME appears to be headed toward Earth, the researchers issue a warning.

Most particles take several days to reach Earth, so there's usually enough time to warn people. But some of a CME's most energetic particles, the ones that can cause the most damage, may reach Earth within a few hours. That short amount of time doesn't give people much time to prepare. Scientists need to learn much more about the sun, its corona, and CMEs.

Putting It All Together

This picture was made by combining three images taken at the same time by different SOHO instruments. The innermost image was taken by the EIT. This image shows the sun's active regions and coronal holes.

The C2 coronagraph has a wider field of view than the EIT. The image of the corona it made is shown just outside the coronagraph's disk.

The C3 coronagraph made the image shown outside the C2 image. The C3 coronagraph has a field of view up to 32 times the width of the sun.

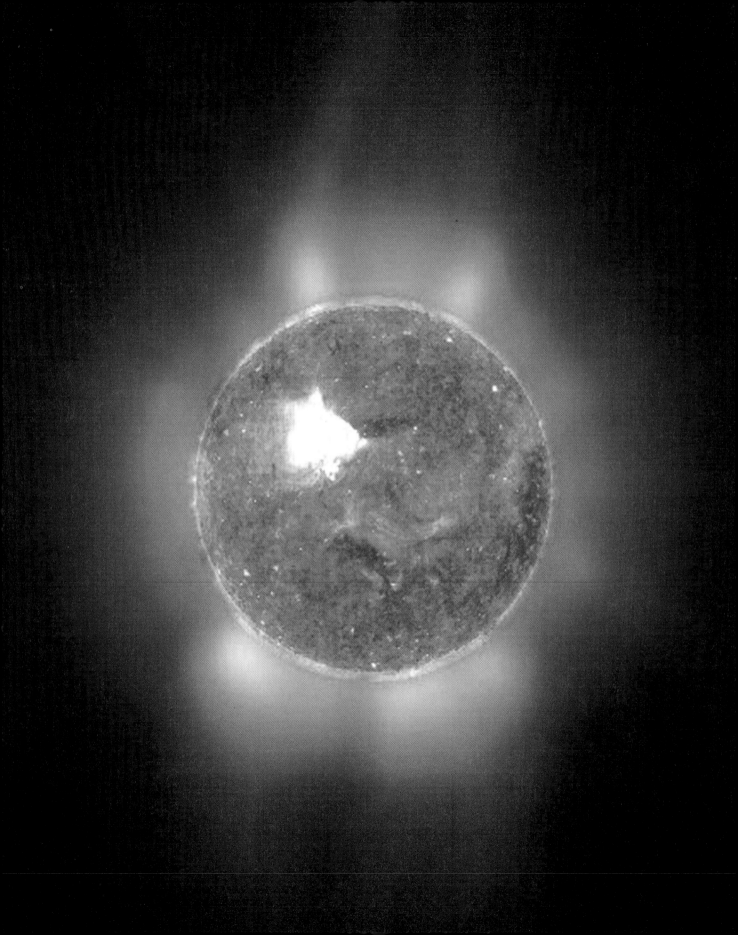

6

SEEING THE WIND

"One of the first things we did with the instrument on SOHO was make the first image in ultraviolet light of the sun's atmosphere."—John Kohl

As new instruments are built to study the sun, new discoveries are made. The biggest advances have come as a result of instruments carried by satellites such as SOHO. Because SOHO operates far from Earth, it can view the sun continuously over long periods of time. And because its specialized equipment can look at the sun in many different kinds of light, many aspects of the sun's behavior have been seen for the first time.

John Kohl, a scientist at the CfA, has been in charge of creating a series of special instruments to view the sun from space. The instruments gather information about a region called the extended solar corona. This region can be seen from Earth in visible light during a total solar eclipse. The extended corona begins more than 700,000 kilometers (about 450,000 miles) above the photosphere. It extends outward into space for millions of kilometers.

John's instruments collect data from the extended solar corona to help create models of the formation of the solar wind. The solar wind is made of streams of charged particles that are ejected from the sun and travel outward into space. "We need to find out about this process in detail before we can predict how solar wind emissions will occur and how they will vary over time," explains John.

One instrument John and others created to study the extended solar corona is called an Ultraviolet Coronagraph Spectrometer (UVCS). A UVCS is carried aboard the SOHO satellite.

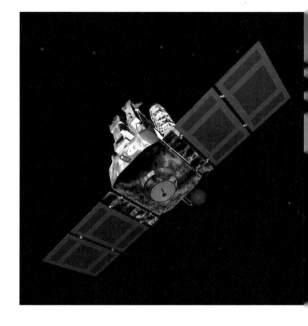

(above)
SOHO was launched into orbit from the Cape Canaveral Air Station, in Cape Canaveral, Florida, on December 2, 1995.

(left)
SOHO took images of ultraviolet light given off by the sun's corona over 27 days. The images were combined to make this single picture. Scientists use SOHO images like this one to study the solar wind.

53

Shaped by the Solar Wind

Scientists' models show that the magnetic field surrounding a planet affects the motion of charged particles that are in a region around the planet. That region is called the magnetosphere. Observations show that most of the charged particles in the solar wind do not penetrate Earth's magnetosphere. Instead, the particles mostly flow around our magnetosphere, the way water flows around a rock in a river.

The solar wind's charged particles change the shape of Earth's magnetosphere. The solar wind "squashes" the magnetosphere on the side that faces the sun. On Earth's other side, the wind "drags" the magnetosphere out into a long tail. The artist's drawing below shows a model of how this may look.

And it's not just Earth that's affected. The solar wind also changes the shapes of the magnetospheres of other planets in the solar system.

Note: Objects in the picture are not drawn to scale.

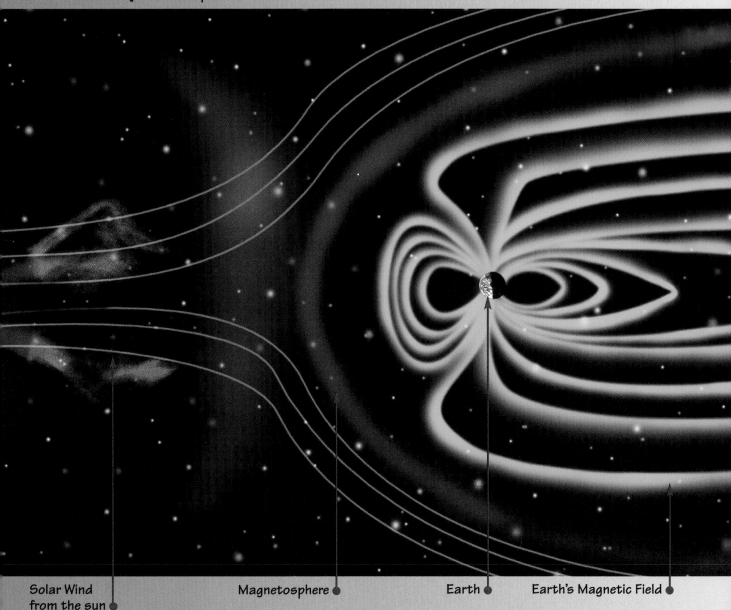

Solar Wind from the sun

Magnetosphere

Earth

Earth's Magnetic Field

Seeing the Sun in a New Light

The UVCS has detectors that can "see" extreme ultraviolet light, or light with some of the shortest wavelengths in the ultraviolet range. John recalls one of the first observations the UVCS sent back from the SOHO satellite. It was the first image ever made in ultraviolet light of the sun's extended corona. "This was very exciting," he says. "We had never seen this part of the sun in this light before."

By studying these images, scientists have learned about the structure of the outer part of the corona. "The appearance of this region depends on the color of the light we use to observe it," says John. "Structures we had observed in visible light, which we thought we could describe, looked much different in ultraviolet light." The ultraviolet light made parts of the extended corona visible for the first time.

John Kohl led a team to build another UVCS that travels to space for shorter periods of time. It travels aboard a small satellite launched from and then retrieved by a space shuttle. Here, John is shown aboard the Space Shuttle Discovery, shortly before the UVCS traveled into space in 1998. Though John did not fly in the shuttle, he went on board before it launched to check that the instrument would operate properly.

Another exciting discovery made possible by UVCS observations is that some of the charged particles in the corona are much hotter than anyone ever thought. "We thought the temperature of the corona would be about 1,000,000° C (about 1,800,000° F)," says John. This estimate came from experiments done using visible light. But once it was possible to study pictures of the corona made in the ultraviolet range, John and others realized that some of the charged particles in the corona are as hot as 200,000,000° or 300,000,000° C (about 360,000,000° or 540,000,000° F). That's more than ten times hotter than the sun's core!

"This was a spectacular finding that we never imagined would happen," says John. The discovery is helping scientists learn more about how the charged particles that make up the solar wind are heated and pushed from the sun. "There were so few ways we could imagine making charged particles that hot," says John. Scientists want to use even more powerful equipment to observe the sun. They want to find out why the charged particles that make up the fast solar wind move so quickly.

New Eyes in the Sky

John is leading a team that hopes to build more powerful instruments to launch aboard a new satellite. This satellite would help scientists gather more data about solar winds. The new satellite, called the Advanced Solar Coronal Explorer (ASCE), would be launched in the next few years. It would carry two instruments that, when combined, would be much more powerful than any instruments flown so far to observe the extended

It's a Breeze.

Xing Li is another scientist at the CfA who studies the solar wind. Xing is especially interested in a type of solar wind that is called the fast solar wind. The fast solar wind is thought to move at speeds of 600 to 1,000 kilometers (about 375 to 620 miles) per second.

Xing wants to find out about how the fast solar wind begins. He often works with observations made by the SOHO satellite.

Before SOHO, scientists could only collect data on the fast solar wind close to Earth. With SOHO, they can now gather information much closer to the sun. Xing and others are using this information to create better models of the fast solar wind.

solar corona. John hopes the new instruments will help scientists gather information to come up with new models to help them predict the behavior of the solar wind. "That is my goal for the rest of my career," he says.

Scientists are always trying to improve their models of the sun's behavior. There is still so much to learn. To find the secrets of the sun, Shadia, Sallie, Leon, Margarita, John, Xing, and many other scientists must work long hours in their laboratories and in observatories. They share their work and puzzle over the results. "I'm just doing a tiny, tiny bit," Shadia says. "There's so much about the sun left to be discovered."

This image of the sun was made by the EIT and UVCS instruments aboard SOHO. The image outside the black ring was made by UVCS. It shows a portion of the extended solar corona in ultraviolet light. Scientists will continue to study images, such as this one, from space and from Earth to learn more about the outer parts of the sun.

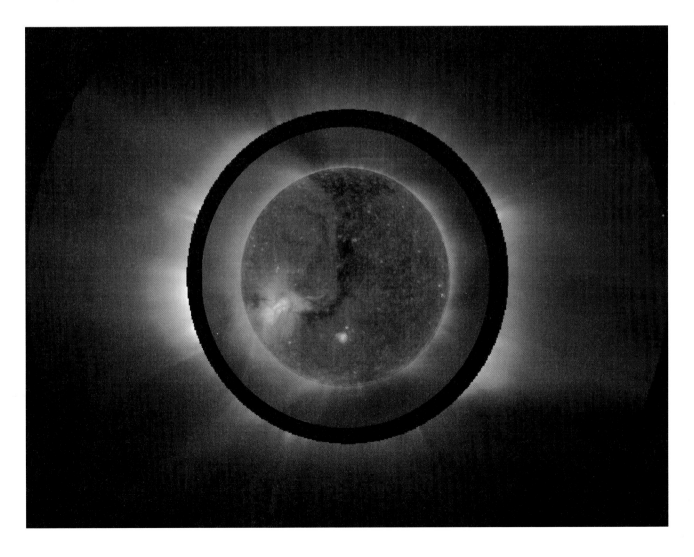

The shimmering lights of auroras are visible from Earth's surface and from above Earth. This picture was taken from space. The inset picture was taken from Earth.

Auroras and Comet Tails

Scientists think solar winds play a part in the formation of beautiful auroras that can sometimes be seen near Earth's poles. Auroras look like faint curtains, streamers, or hazy, colored lights that seem to dance across the night sky.

Solar winds may also shape and direct the electrically charged parts of comet tails. Comets often have two tails. One is made of dust. The other, not always visible, is made of ions, or individual, electrically charged atoms or molecules. This second tail is sometimes called the comet's "ion tail." Comets' tails point away from the sun.

This is a picture of comet Hale-Bopp. The comet's dust tail is on the top. The comet's ion tail is on the bottom.

When photographing the sun on June 1 and 2, 1998, the SOHO spacecraft made a picture that shows two comets (visible at bottom right of the picture). Notice that the comets' dust tails point away from the sun. The coronagraph's disk in the middle of the picture blocks the sun's light so that fainter, nearby objects can be seen. The white circle shows the location of the edge of the photosphere.

GLOSSARY

auroras Also known as the northern and southern lights. Auroras are streaks of glowing gas caused by charged particles from the solar wind trapped in Earth's magnetic field.

chromosphere The region that extends about 2,000 kilometers (about 1,300 miles) above the photosphere.

corona The outer part of the sun. The corona can only be seen with the naked eye during a total solar eclipse.

coronagraph A device used to help study the sun's corona. It has a disk that blocks the photosphere. This device makes it possible to photograph the sun's corona with other instruments.

Coronal Mass Ejection (CME) A sudden release of millions of tons of electrically charged particles from the sun into space.

density The amount of matter in a specific quantity of space.

eclipse The blocking of light by an object. In a solar eclipse, the moon is between Earth and the sun, and blocks the sun's light.

eclipse path The area on Earth's surface covered by the moon's shadow during a solar eclipse.

extended solar corona The area of the corona that begins at a distance greater than 700,000 kilometers (420,000 miles) above the photosphere. It extends outward into space for millions of kilometers.

extreme ultraviolet light Light with the shortest wavelengths in the ultraviolet range.

gamma rays The type of light with the shortest wavelengths.

magnetic field A model scientists use to help describe the effects of magnets on the motions of charged particles.

magnetosphere The region around a planet controlled by the planet's magnetic field.

model A description used to explain something. Models are used to predict nature's behavior.

photosphere The apparent surface of the sun.

prominence A huge loop of hot gas that arches between two sunspots.

radio waves Light with the longest wavelengths.

solar wind Streams of electrically charged particles that are ejected from the sun and travel outward into space.

sunspots Irregularly shaped dark spots on the sun's surface.

totality The short period of time when the moon completely covers the photosphere of the sun during a total solar eclipse seen from Earth.

ultraviolet Light that has wavelengths shorter than visible light. Spending too much time in this kind of light can cause sunburn.

visible light Light that we can see with our eyes.

X-rays A type of light with wavelengths that are shorter than the wavelengths of ultraviolet light and longer than the wavelengths of gamma rays.

FURTHER READING

Beasant, Pam. *1000 Facts About Space*. New York, NY: Kingfisher Books, 1992.

Burton, Jane, and Kim Taylor. *The Nature and Science of Sunlight*. Exploring the Science of Nature. Milwaukee, WI: Gareth Stevens, 1997.

Datnow, Claire L. *Edwin Hubble: Discoverer of Galaxies*. Great Minds of Science. Springfield, NJ: Enslow Publishers, 1997.

Estalella, Robert. *Our Star: The Sun*. Windows on the Universe. Hauppauge, NY: Barron's Educational Series, 1993.

Gardner, Robert. *Science Project Ideas About the Sun*. Springfield, NJ: Enslow Publishers, 1997.

Grimshaw, Caroline, ed. *Sun*. Chicago, IL: World Book, Inc., 1998.

VanCleave, Janice P. *Janice VanCleave's Astronomy for Every Kid: 101 Easy Experiments That Really Work*. New York, NY: John Wiley & Sons, 1991.

INDEX

Acknowledgments

We offer special thanks to Dr. Irwin Shapiro, Director of the Harvard-Smithsonian Center for Astrophysics, who took a particular interest in this series, and made time in a very crowded schedule to work closely with us to ensure the material's accuracy and completeness. Thanks also to Brenda Bernard, Susan Brams, Audrey Bryant, Virginia Downes, Barbara Foster, Mary Gregory, Steele Hill, Meg Kassakian, Deborah Kovacs, Zdravko Kristic, Amy Pallant, Nayla Rathle, Tania Ruiz, Matt Schneps, Susan Sherman, Sally Sisson, Sally Stephens, and Erica Thrall. We also wish to gratefully acknowledge the help and support of the following people who were interviewed for this book: Leon Golub, Shadia Habbal, Margarita Karovska, John Kohl, and Xing Li. We would particularly like to thank Sallie Baliunas for her generous help over the course of the book's development.

Credits

AURA/NOAO/NSF: 19 insets; Baliunas, Sallie: 45 middle; The British Museum: 3 top, 15; Brown, Todd/National Solar Observatory, Sacramento Peak: 41; CfA: 42 inset, 55; Chase, Jon: 24, 49; Corbis/Carig Aurness: 14; Corbis/Werner H. Muller: 34; Espenek, Fred: 4, 12–13 inset, 13 bottom, 28; Fletcher, Bill, and Sally: 59 top; High Altitude Observatory Archives: 47; Golub, Leon: 22; Golub, Leon, and Serge Koutchney: 25; Habbal, Shadia: 6, 7; Halevi, Marcus: 2 right, 45, 56; High Altitude Observatory, National Center for Atmospheric Research (NCAR), Boulder, CO: 20, 21; Houghton Library/Harvard University: 33, 45 left; Hutchinson, Dick: 58 inset; Lockheed Martin: 18–19, 30–31; Lunar and Planetary Institute: 12–13 background; NASA: 2 left, 9, 10, 35, 58 background; NASA Goddard Space Flight Center: 1 inset, 26; National Maritime Museum Picture Library: 44; National Solar Observatory/Sacramento Peak: 32, 43; Padilla, Steve/Mount Wilson Observatory: 42 bottom; Observatories of the Carnegie Institution of Washington: 40; Royal Astronomical Society: 8; SOHO, a project of international cooperation between ESA and NASA: 3 bottom, 53, 54; SOHO/EIT consortium: 2 middle, 29, 46, 50, 52; SOHO/LASCO consortium: 48, 51, 59 bottom; SOHO/MDI consortium: 38, 39; SOHO/UVCS/EIT consortium: 57; Stanford-Lockheed Insitute for Space Research/NASA Small Explorer Program: 27; U.S. Army White Sands Missle Range: 23.

Illustration on page 5 is by Jill Leichter.

Illustration on page 9 is by Heidi Wormser.

Illustration on page 17 is by Michael Carroll.